★
THE
BIG
TIME

JUSTIN BIEBER

AARON FRISCH

CREATIVE EDUCATION

JUSTIN BIEBER

TABLE OF CONTENTS

MEET JUSTIN

When Justin takes the stage, the crowd screams. When he smiles and points at his fans, they scream louder. And when he begins to spin and sing, the *arena* gets louder yet!

Justin Bieber is one of the most famous pop stars in the world. He is known for his catchy songs. Justin became famous for his hair-style, too. His fans say they have "Bieber Fever"!

Justin likes to meet and thank his fans at shows

JUSTIN'S CHILDHOOD

Justin was born March 1, 1994, in London, Ontario. His mom raised him by herself. Justin spent a lot of time with his grandparents, too. The Bieber family was very religious.

Justin with his mom, Pattie, before an awards show in 2011

LONDON, ONTARIO, CANADA

GETTING INTO MUSIC

As a young boy, Justin liked hockey and soccer. He liked music even more. His mom gave him a drum set when he was two. Justin taught himself how to play the drums, piano, and guitar.

Besides singing, Justin plays many instruments

When he was 12, Justin performed in singing contests. His mom made videos of him and put them on YouTube. A music *agent* saw his videos. Soon, Justin went to Atlanta, Georgia, to record music.

Justin was 15 when he performed on Good Morning America *in 2009*

THE BIG TIME

When Justin released his song "Baby" in 2010, he became a *teen idol*. Girls especially went crazy over his music. They collected pictures of Justin and watched all his music videos.

....

Most of the loudest fans at Justin's concerts are girls

Justin *toured* the United States and Canada. He became an actor, too. In 2011, a movie called *Never Say Never* came out. It was about Justin's life and showed him singing during concerts.

. . . .

Justin sang for a crowd before a showing of Never Say Never *in 2011*

OFF THE STAGE

When he is not on the stage, Justin likes to play sports and hang out with his friends. He has dated actress and singer Selena Gomez. Justin spends a lot of time in the U.S., but he is still a *citizen* of Canada.

Justin with friends on a roller coaster (left); Selena Gomez (right)

WHAT IS NEXT?

By 2011, Justin's voice began to sound deeper. That year, he made a new Christmas album called *Under the Mistletoe*. Justin turned 18 in 2012. He is not a kid anymore, but he is still a hit with his young fans!

....

Justin won many awards in his first years as a star

WHAT JUSTIN SAYS ABOUT ...

DREAMS

"Follow your dreams and don't let anyone stop you. Never say never."

GROWING UP

"I think I can grow as an artist, and my fans will grow with me."

HIS VOICE CHANGING

"It cracks. Like every teenage boy, I'm dealing with it.... Some of the notes I hit on 'Baby' I can't hit anymore."

GLOSSARY

agent someone who finds talented people like singers and then helps them get work

arena a large building with many seats that holds sports events or concerts

citizen a person who lives in or belongs to a certain city, state, or country

teen idol a teenage entertainer who becomes so famous that almost everyone knows who he or she is

toured traveled to different cities within a country or around the world to do concerts

READ MORE

Gosman, Gillian. *Justin Bieber*. New York: Powerkids, 2012.

Tieck, Sarah. *Justin Bieber: Pop Music Superstar*. Minneapolis: Abdo, 2012.

WEB SITES

Justin Bieber Biography
http://www.people.com/people/justin_bieber/
This site has information about Justin's life and many pictures, too.

Justin Bieber Music
http://www.justinbiebermusic.com/
This is Justin's own Web site, with news and messages from Justin.

INDEX

PUBLISHED BY Creative Education
P.O. Box 227, Mankato, Minnesota 56002
Creative Education is an imprint of The Creative Company
www.thecreativecompany.us

DESIGN AND PRODUCTION BY Christine Vanderbeek
ART DIRECTION BY Rita Marshall
PRINTED IN the United States of America

PHOTOGRAPHS BY Alamy (Everett Collection Inc.), Dreamstime (Aaron Settipane), Getty Images (John Blanding/The Boston Globe, Gilbert Carrasquillo/FilmMagic, Rick Diamond/CMT, Jeff Kravitz/FilmMagic, Mathew Imaging/WireImage, Kevin Mazur/WireImage, Ethan Miller/ABC), iStockphoto (GYI NSEA, Pingebat, Cole Vineyard), Shutterstock (Helga Esteb, Featureflash, MillaF)

LIBRARY OF CONGRESS CATALOGING-IN-PUBLICATION DATA
Frisch, Aaron.
Justin Bieber / Aaron Frisch.
p. cm. — (The big time)
Includes bibliographical references and index.
Summary: An elementary introduction to the life, work, and popularity of Justin Bieber, a Canadian pop singer who became known as a teen idol and gained fame with such songs as "Baby."

ISBN 978-1-60818-330-2
1. Bieber, Justin, 1994- —Juvenile literature. 2. Singers—Canada—Biography—Juvenile literature. I. Title.
ML3930.B54F75 2013
782.42164092—dc23 [B]   2012013644

First edition
9 8 7 6 5 4 3 2 1